639.3 Armentrout, David
ARM   Rusty Wallace

T0072770

RUSTY WALLACE

IN THE FAST LANE

David and Patricia Armentrout

Rourke

Publishing LLC

Vero Beach, Florida 32964

www.rourkepublishing.com

PHOTO CREDITS: Title pg. ©Autostock; all other photos ©Getty Images

Title page: *Rusty Wallace pits the #2 Miller Lite Dodge.*

Editor: Robert Stengard-Olliges

Cover design by Nicola Stratford

Library of Congress Cataloging-in-Publication Data

Armentrout, David, 1962-
  Rusty Wallace : in the fast lane / David and Patricia Armentrout.
    p. cm. -- (In the fast lane)
  Includes index.
  ISBN 1-60044-220-X (hardcover)
  ISBN 978-1-60044-313-8 (paperback)
  1. Wallace, Rusty, 1955 or 6---Juvenile literature. 2. Stock car
drivers--United States--Biography--Juvenile literature. I. Armentrout,
Patricia, 1960- II. Title. III. Series.
  GV1032.W35A75 2007
  796.72092--dc22
                              2006010684

Printed in the USA

CG/CG

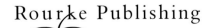

Rourke Publishing

www.rourkepublishing.com – sales@rourkepublishing.com
Post Office Box 3328, Vero Beach, FL 32964

TABLE OF CONTENTS

RUSTY WALLACE

Rusty Wallace is as comfortable in the cockpit of a **stock car** as most people are in their favorite chair. Flying around the track at speeds reaching more than 200 miles an hour may sound crazy to some, but it's all in a days work for Rusty.

Born: August 14, 1956
Organization: NASCAR
Car: Dodge #2
Car owner: Roger Penske
Team: Penske Racing
Sponsor: Miller Lite

Kurt Busch drafts behind leader Rusty Wallace at Pocono Raceway in Pennsylvania.

A RACING LEGEND

Rusty Wallace is one of the greatest drivers in the history of **NASCAR**. Rusty began racing stock cars full time in NASCAR's famed Winston Cup series (now the Nextel Cup) in 1984. It immediately became clear, Rusty was an elite driver. Rusty did not win any races that year, but he did post four top-ten finishes. Good enough to win NASCAR's **Rookie** of the Year.

Rusty at the Daytona 500 during his 1984 rookie year.

CHECKERED FLAG

It's one thing to compete in stock car's most challenging racing circuit, but it's another to actually win a race. Rusty was determined. He took his first checkered flag in 1986 at Bristol Motor Speedway in Tennessee. He won his second race that same year at Martinsville Speedway in Virginia. By the end of the year, he was ranked sixth in the Winston Cup point standings.

Rusty poses for photos after his ninth career win at Bristol Motor Speedway in 2000.

FAST FACTS

The first driver to pass the black and white checkered flag wins the race.

CLIMBING TO THE TOP

Rusty won two more races in 1987 and climbed even higher in the point standings, finishing fifth. But Rusty wasn't satisfied. He had tasted victory and was gaining confidence in his ability to win. His goal was to win a Winston Cup **championship**.

1988 brought him even closer to his goal. Six wins and 19 top-five finishes earned Rusty his best finish so far. He finished second in the point standings, just 24 points behind driver Bill Elliott.

Rusty and crew complete a final inspection prior to a race.

WINSTON CUP CHAMPIONSHIP

By 1989, Rusty was an established driver in the Winston Cup series. Everything seemed to be going right. Rusty finished the year with six victories and 20 top-ten finishes. Still, the season came down to the wire. Rusty narrowly defeated Dale Earnhardt Sr. winning the Winston Cup championship by 12 points.

Rusty in the #27 Kodiak car at the 1989 Daytona 500.

FAST FACTS

NASCAR Point System for Each Race

Winner	driver earns 180 points
Runner-up	driver earns 170 points
3rd-6th position	points drop in 5-point increments (3rd position-165 points, 4th-160, 5th-155, and 6th-150 points)
7th-11th position	points drop in 4-point increments
12th-42nd position	points drop in 3-point increments
Last place	driver earns 34 points

**Drivers can earn bonus points for leading
a lap and leading the most laps**

*Rusty and Sterling
Marlin unwind after a
1995 qualifying heat.*

A WINNING TRADITION

Since winning his first Winston Cup race in 1986, Rusty has had remarkable success. Rusty has driven himself to the top-five in the final standings seven times. In a stretch that lasted from 1986 through 2002, Rusty failed to finish a season in the top-ten only once.

Rusty has won 55 Cup races and is ranked ninth in all-time career wins. All that success has earned Rusty a nice paycheck. He is fourth on the all-time career money list, having earned well over 43 million dollars.

Rusty leads the pack at Watkins Glen National Raceway.

A TOUGH COMPETITOR

There are four major types of tracks in the Nextel Cup circuit. Each track has its own characteristics. Rusty has won races on the majority of them.

During his career, he has posted multiple wins on many of NASCAR's toughest courses. Rusty is best known for his talent on short tracks. Short track racing is non-stop action pitting drivers against each other in a test of nerves. Nearly half of Rusty's wins have come on short tracks.

Rusty pulls double duty, racing the #64 Miller Dodge in NASCAR's Busch series.

NEED FOR SPEED

Does Rusty ever slow down? Not Really. Rusty's love for speed carries over to his personal life. Rusty is not only a racecar driver, he is also an accomplished pilot. When time allows, Rusty takes to the skies in the cockpit of one of his airplanes. Rusty even has his own helicopter.

FAST FACTS

Rusty has crashed his car many times during his career, but he says his most embarrassing accident occurred after winning a race in Springfield, Missouri. Rusty crashed in front of a cheering crowd during his victory lap around the track.

Rusty Wallace is one of the greatest drivers in the history of NASCAR.

DOWNSHIFTING

Rusty's career has been nothing less than a dream come true. But the hectic schedule of races, appearances, and never ending events has left little time for family and other interests. Although he will stay involved in stock car racing, Rusty decided that 2005 would be his last year as a full-time Nextel Cup driver. His fans will no doubt miss watching one of the greatest drivers in NASCAR history.

Career Highlights

2005: Finished eighth in points in his final year as a full time NASCAR driver

2001: Finished his 16th straight year with at least one Winston Cup victory

1993: Won ten Winston Cup races, finished second in point standings

1989: Won the Winston Cup championship

1988: Finished second in the Winston Cup point standings

1986: Won his first Winston Cup race

1984: Won NASCAR's Rookie of the Year

GLOSSARY

championship (CHAM pee uhn ship) — each driver is awarded points in a race, with winners earning the most. The driver with the most points at the end of a season wins the championship

NASCAR — National Association for Stock Car Auto Racing: the governing body for the Nextel Cup, Craftsman Truck, and Busch series, among others

rookie (ROOK ee) — a first-year driver

stock car (STOK KAR) — a commercially available car that has been modified for racing

INDEX

FURTHER READING

Gigliotti, Jim. Kelley, K.C. *NASCAR, Authorized Handbook.*
    Reader's Digest Children's Books, 2004.
Burt, William. *NASCAR's Best: Stock Car Racing's Top Drivers.*
    Motorbooks International, 2004.

WEBSITES TO VISIT

www.rustywallace.com
www.nascar.com
www.penskeracing.com

ABOUT THE AUTHORS

David and Patricia Armentrout have written many nonfiction books for young readers. They have had several books published for primary school reading. The Armentrouts live in Cincinnati, Ohio, with their two children.